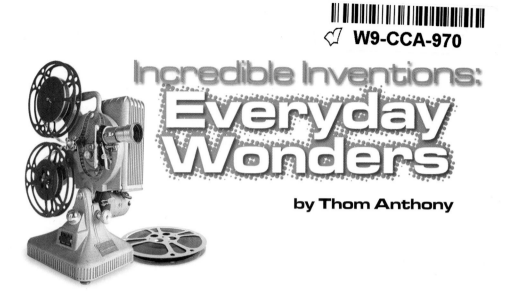

Incredible Inventions: Everyday Wonders

by Thom Anthony

Table of Contents

Introduction

Think of a world with none of the familiar objects that make life easy. Can you picture life without lights? How about life without TVs or phones? It seems as if we've always had these things, but that's not true. It's only recently that some everyday objects were invented.

↻ Long ago, people had to use candles for light as in this painting from 1650.

⬆ Today, lights can be found all over.

Before you were born, phones were not as easy to use as they are today. **Electric** light bulbs weren't as bright as they are today. The first TVs had tubes that would burn out.

People keep looking for smart ways to make things work better. They keep finding ways to make life easier.

Chapter 1
Light

Long ago people used fire for light. Fire burns very quickly, and the light from fire is not very bright.

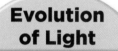

Evolution of Light

Fire Light

Candle Light

Gas Light

A Bright Idea

In 1991 a new kind of light bulb was made. It could provide light for as long as 10,000 hours.

Things changed when the electric light bulb was invented in the 1870s.

A man named Thomas Alva Edison (1847–1931) made one of the first light bulbs. Soon bulbs were being used everywhere.

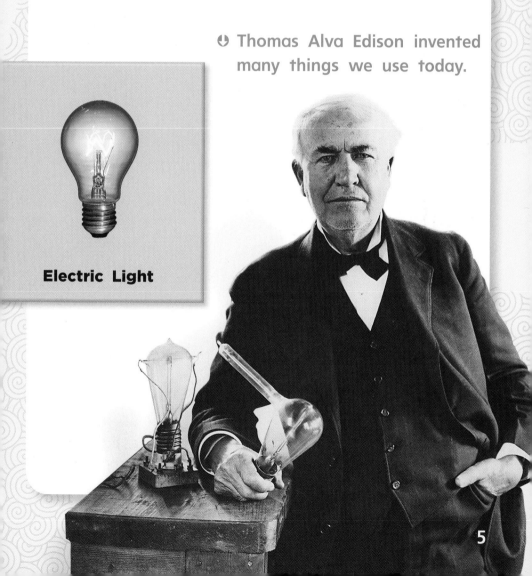

↻ Thomas Alva Edison invented many things we use today.

Electric Light

Chapter 2

Listening

Once people who lived far apart could only write letters to share ideas. Then the first telephone was invented. People had a faster way to keep in touch.

The first telephones needed cords to make them work, but now many phones don't have them. Telephones used to have **rotary** dials that you turned with your finger. Now most telephones have buttons.

The Telephone

The First Telephone

Rotary Telephone

Touchtone Telephone

Today, we can even use the telephone to send written messages. This is called a fax.

AMAZING INVENTIONS

The Telegraph

Before telephones, the telegraph was used to send messages. The telegraph uses the Morse code to spell letters and words.

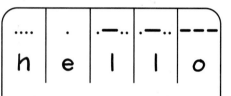

⊙ This is in Morse code. Each group of dots and dashes stands for a letter.

Cordless Phone

Fax Machine

Cell Phone

Long ago people did not listen to music on a tape or CD. They had to go to a place where music was being played. Then a way was found to record sound. First, songs were recorded on tin foil. The foil was wrapped around what looked like a tin can. Then the recording was played on a phonograph.

◔ Thomas Alva Edison invented one of the first phonographs.

The CD is a popular ⮑
way to store music.

Next, large flat discs called records were used to store sound. Some people disliked them because they could get scratched, and scratches caused skips in the music. Next, small cassette tapes that didn't scratch were used. CDs, small discs that can store a lot of music, were the next invention.

The MP3 Player

Today, songs can be stored in computer files called MP3s. A tiny MP3 player can hold many hours of music.

Chapter 3
Looking

The first movies didn't have sound or color. Instead, words flashed on the screen to tell people what the actors were saying. Pictures were in shades of black and white.

↺ Actors in silent films had to get their messages across with their faces and gestures.

↺ This movie projector was used years ago.

Now, movies have **special effects**. These effects help the movie look more real or very unreal. Computers can create special effects that make us think there is a terrible storm. They can make us believe a UFO is landing. They can even make a person appear to be flying.

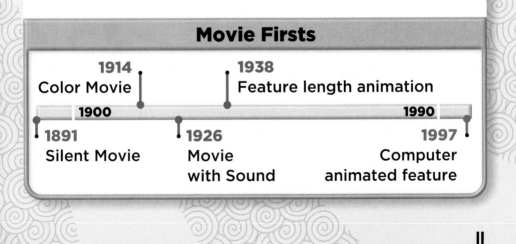

Movie Firsts

1914
Color Movie

1938
Feature length animation

1900

1990

1891
Silent Movie

1926
Movie
with Sound

1997
Computer
animated feature

Before color TVs, families watched entertainment on small black and white screens. People didn't have TV remote controls. They'd use a dial on the TV to change the channel, and there were very few channels to select from.

This TV set was ➲ used in the 1940s.

◔ Now there are many kinds of TVs that have flat screens.

The VCR

A machine called the VCR came out in 1976. It could play movies recorded on a tape. It could also record and play back TV shows.

Today, there are many channels. TVs are better made. They have clearer pictures and excellent sound. They come in many sizes, and most have remote controls. Many of the new TVs also have built-in speakers that make you feel like you are in a theater.

Conclusion

Inventions have made our lives easier and more fun. The things we use now will be improved and made to work even better in the future.

Someday you may use a **robot** to help you clean your room or to cut the grass. You may touch a pad on your door, and it will open for you. You won't even need a key. Can you make some predictions about new inventions? Maybe one of your predictions will be the next everyday wonder.

Glossary

electric *(i-LEK-trik)* something that is powered by a source of energy called electricity *(page 3)*

robot *(ROH-bot)* a machine that can do work in place of a human being *(page 14)*

rotary *(ROH-tuh-ree)* turning or built to turn around on its axis *(page 6)*

special effects *(SPESH-uhl i-FEKTS)* things used in movies to make them look or sound more real or unreal *(page 11)*

Index

Comprehension Check

Summarize

Use the photographs in the book to summarize what you learned about inventions.

Think and Compare

1. Turn to page 9 in this book. Why didn't some people like to use records for entertainment? *(Evaluate Fact and Opinion)*

2. Which objects discussed in this book do you use the most at home or school? In what ways would your life be different without them? *(Apply)*

3. How has the world changed because of the inventions mentioned in this book? Explain. *(Evaluate)*